VLADIMIR MAYAKOVSKY: A TRAGEDY

T0036868

Vladimir
Mayakovsky

Vladimir Mayakovsky: A Tragedy
A Futurist Play in Verse

Translated from the Russian by
Paul Schmidt

Drawings by
Vladimir Mayakovsky and David Burliuk

GREEN INTEGER
KØBENHAVN & LOS ANGELES
2018

GREEN INTEGER
Edited by Per Bregne
København / Los Angeles
(323) 937-3783 / www.greeninteger.com

Distributed in the United States by
Consortium Book Sales & Distribution / Ingram Books
(800) 283-3572 / www.cbsd.com

First Green Integer Edition 2018
English translation copyright ©2018 by Paul Schmidt
Artwork ©2018 by Vladimir Mayakovsky and David Burliuk
Back cover copy ©2018 by Green Integer
All rights reserved

Book design: Guy Bennett & Pablo Capra
Cover photograph: Vladimir Mayakovsky

LIBRARY OF CONGRESS CATALOGING-IN-PUBLICATION DATA
Vladimir Mayakovsky [1893-1930]
Vladimir Mayakovsky
ISBN: 978-1-55713-444-8
p. cm – Green Integer 219
I. Title II. Series III. Translator

Green Integer books are published for Douglas Messerli
Printed in the USA

Contents

Cast of Characters...........................8

Prologue....................................9

Act One....................................13

Act Two....................................37

Epilogue...................................49

About the Author...........................52

Vladimir Mayakovsky: A Tragedy

*in Two Acts
with a Prologue and an Epilogue*

Cast of Characters

Vladimir Vladimirovich Mayakovsky, a poet, 20-25
    years old
An enormous woman, friend of his, maybe twenty
    feet tall, never says a thing
An old man with scrawny black cats, a couple of
    thousand years old
A man with one eye and one leg
A man with one ear
A man with no head
A woman who cries ordinary tears
A woman who cries little tiny tears
A woman who cries great big tears
A man with a long face
An ordinary young man
Little paper boys and girls
Little baby kisses, etc.

Prologue
Mayakovsky

Can you understand why I am **silent**

In this whirlwind of sneers

And carry my **soul** like food on a platter

Toward the coming years

On the stone **stubble** of the public *pavement*

I slide like unnecessary **tears**

I am a **poet** and I am possibly

HAVE YOU SEEN the bruises on the faces of **boredom**

Hanging over **pathways** of stone

And the iron arms of bridges that arch and twist

Through soap-sud rage on the slippery necks

Of foaming streams?

Above me the heavens weep harshly

They jangle above me!

And a **slit-mouth** cloud has the twisted look

Of a woman **expecting a** bab Y

When what she got was a mongoloid from God.

You are **stung** by the sun with his great fat **fingers!**

They are covered all over with little **red** hairs!

They are worse than the whine of sadistic mosquitoes!

Your *souls* are his slaves, his kisses have killed them!

I hate the **light** of day, I always have.

My hatred is fearless, my hatred advances,

My soul is a filament, stretched like the **nerves** of
    a wire:

I'm the king of street light land!

Come unto me all you *WHO* shatter the silence

Who scream at the nooses of noon about your
    necks!

My words are simple as a blow-job,

Self-evident soul-suck, with sounds

That burn **LIKE** street lights.

Feel my fingers move upon **your head**.

Your lips will swell for **gorgeou**s kisses

And the **TONGUES** of all nations will be as
    your ow N.

And what about me, bright, shining me?

I'll dissolve in the distance

Like a little lost soul,

Descend to my throne through crumbling vaults

With holes full of stars.

Bright, shining me!

I will lie down lazy in a **LINEN** sheet

I will make my **bed** in the **shit** of the street

And quietly kiss the knees of the track

While the weight of a freight train

Caresses my back.

Act One
Happy
A city. A spider web
tangle of streets.
Poor people hav-
ing a holiday. V
Mayakovsky alone.
People carry on
food from store
front advertise-
ments. A tin her-
ring from a sign.
A huge gold bagel.
Big pieces of yel-
low velvet.
Mayakovsky

Ladies and gentlemen!

Sew up my soul

So my nothingness won't leak out.

If somebody **spits**

I don't know if that's good

Or that's bad.

I'm as dry as an overworked **w**et **n**urse.

Ladies and gentleme N !

YOUR ATTENTION, PLEASE!

A rising young poet will now do a dance

For your entertainment.

Enter the Old Man
with Scrawny Black
Cats. He pats them.
He is all beard.
Mayakovsky

Ransack the houses, drag out the **fatties**, the
   ones who sit sloshing in their greasy shells,

Beat me out a **RHYTHM** on the drums and the bells!

Gotta tackle the **dumb ones**, the ones that
   can't hear

You gotta WHISTLE down your flute and tickle
   their ears!

Watch me gobble down the brand new bagel of
   a hot idea

And kick out the bottoms of barrels of badness;

Shout congratulations to me loud and clear

Today **I'm** getting married, and I'm **M**arrying **M**adness!

The stage slowly begins to fill with people. Enter the Man with One Ear, the Man without a Head, etc. They move like doped-up druggies in a daze. Everything's a mess. Everybody keeps on eating. Mayakovsky

I'm a **barefoot** jeweler, and I **P**olish my **P**oems

The way you polish your diamonds.

I fluff **feather pillows** in strange people's houses.

I push a button and presto!

Holiday!

All the rich and ragged beggars in the world

Can celebrate **t**oda**y**.

The Old Man with the Cats

I'm an old, old man, **I'm a t**housan**d years** old

And I see you, sonny, I see what you are,

You're a cry of anguish crucified upon a cros**S**
of laugh**S**.

Over the city one enormous sorrow floats

While a hundred **p**iddling little ones spot the sky;

Street lights and head lights meet in a rush,

A clash that **covers** the hesitant hush of dawn.

These flabby old *moons* have lost their *charm*:

Street light now is the trenchant fashion,

Its wit bites harder. Things are in charge.

In the world of cities, **things** run the show.

And things have no souls, they **want** to wipe us
out.

A god gone mad l**oo**ks down out of heaven

At the howls of his **hu**man hordes,

His hands in his beard and his beard in tangles,

White with the dust of dissolving **roads**.

He warns you himself of his Cruel retribution

But you only sigh a silly sigh and scratch your
scabby soul.

Get rid of him! Go pat cats! Pat skinny black cats!

Grab their great big bellies and boast that you've
done it!

Pop the bubble gum bubbles of your city slicker
cheeks!

Only in cats with rainbow coats

CAN YOU FIND the true flash of electric eyes.

Pat them and haul in the harvest of flashes,
streaks

of abundant electric fire.

Let it all stream out! into muscle-tight stretches
of wire!

Streetcars will jump and signals will flame

Night will flare brighter than victory parades!

Amazed at its face in such *radiant* make-up

The world will *shudder* slowly into action.

Flowers in every window will flash their
peacock tails!

People will travel on **cables** and **rails**,

And after them hundreds of cats.

Great fat blue black cats.

This cat and that cat! Pat that cat!

St*ick* **stars** all over the people you love

And decorate dresses with comets and planets

And cats! cats! fat black cats! skinny black cats!

0, forget your apartments and go **pat**

Cats! Go **pat** **fat** black cats!

*The Man with
One Ear.*

Oh, it's tru**E**! look up in the air!

High above the city where **W**eather-vanes
spin

A woman has eyelids darker than caves.

She **covers** the sidewalks with gobs of s*p*it

And the spit goblins grow into great big cripples.

High above the **city** somebody's guilt thickens
  into revenge.

People gather in groups, they STAMPE*DE* in the
  streets.

And there, where win E -stains pattern the
  skies,

An old man slumps at his keyboard and cries.

A crowd gathers.
He continues.

High above the **city**, nothing but suffering, far
  and wide.

You reach for a note, your hands get all bloody.

A piano player's fingers were bitten bad

By the rabid white teeth of a snarling keyboard.

Agitation and alarm.
He goes on.

And now **today**, ever since

This morning,

A fast fandango has *razored* a mouth

In my soul!

I go around twitching with my **arms** raised to
heaven

And the rooftops are covered with chimneys that
dance,

All bent over like the number .

·Ladies and gentlemen, stop!

Is this right?

Even the sidestreets are ready **for** a fight.

And my **longing** for something keeps growing,
I don't know what.

I feel like a tear on the **nose** of a beaten pup.

*Everybody gets
more upset.
The Old Man with
the Cats*

Now **listen** up, folks, we've got us a problem.

We've got to get rid of our **things**.

I told you they weren't to be trusted,

They pretended they loved you
And now look.

*The Man with a
Long Face.*

> But may**be** we just didn't love them enough. You
> gotta
>
> *Love* your things, so they'll love you back.

*The Man with One
Ear.*

> **B**ut lots of things aren't put together ri**ght**.
>
> They can't feel a thing. they've got *blocked*
> emotions.

*The Man with a
Long Face, joyfully
nodding agreement.*

> See, on your face, **where** you have a mouth,
>
> **Lot**s of things have an ear! That's where they
> hear!

*Mayakovsky ap-
pears in the heart of
town.*

> Don't heat up your hearts with the oil of anger.
>
> *You* are all my children. Come learn your lessons.
>
> I am your stern teacher; I spa**re** not the rod.
>
> Remember your places, you people. Who are
> you?

You are tinkling bells on the **fool's cap** of God.

My feet are all swollen with searching.

I have trekked your *country* from end **to** end

I have crossed over other lands as well

In a mask and a cloak—the domino of
      darkness—

I have sought out her **unseen** soul.

i wanted to wipe my wounded lips

with the softness of her healing flowers.

Pause

I have crouched like a slave dripping

Blood and sweat, and rocked
            my wracked body

In mad, mad motion, weeping in misery—

And *one time* I actually found her, the soul of this
      country,

I mean, but she was wearing a dirty blue house
      dress and she **said hi** glad to

see you sit down you **want** some tea?

Pause

I am a poet and I've wiped out the spaces

Between my own face and *other people's faces*:

In the pus and abcesses of city **morgues**

I've gone to discover my soul's sister;

I've covered sick people with passionate kisses

And today on a bonfire's yellow flame

Deeper than the hid**de**n tears of the **SEA**

I will throw my sister's secret shame

And your gray-haired mothers' wr**inkl**ed faces.

And on plates licked clean in fancy places

We **will** gorge on the meat of eternity.

He rips away a
veil. The Enormous
Woman. Everyone
crowds around her
in a panic. The
Ordinary Young
Man rushes in.
Much ado.
Mayakovsky con-
tinues.

Ladies and gentlemen, don't get hysterical.

The word is out, and the word is this:

Somewhere—I think it's in South America—

One happy man r**eally** d**oe**s exist.

The   Ordinary
Young Man.
He runs around
grabbing people by
their lapels.

Listen here, **everybody**,

Listen, lady, listen, miste**R**,

Wait a minute, wait a minute,

What the hell is going on?

Is **this** the place I heard of

Where you're all opposed to motherhood?

Listen, that's downright illegal!

You think you know all the answers

But you're nuthin next to nature.

You people—

You just wanna start a riot

And destroy the things we've worked for!

Listen here, I been to college

—that should prove I'm not a dummy—

Wanna hear what **I invented**?

A machine for slicing meat-loaf!

And **I g**ott**a** friend who's working

On a trap for catching fleas!

Well, all *right!*

And I gotta little **WOMAN**

And we're gonna have a baby,

So let's not have any trouble!

Now to me you **DON'T LOOK STUPID**

But the things you say are crazY—

And it really is a **goddam** shame.

The Man with
One Ear

Young **man**, why don't you get up on this

soap-box here...

A voice from the
crowd.

Better he should go down on it!

The Man with
One Ear

...So everyone can see yo**U** .

The Ordinary
Young Man

What's so funny? What's so funny?

Look, *I* gotta little brother,

Just a baby, but you people—

Whaddaya want? Whaddaya want?

You'll go gobble gobble gobble

And you'll eat up all his bones.

Alarms, automo-
bile horns, crowds
murmuring:

Pants

Pants

Pants

Pants

Pants

Mayakovsky

Knock it off!

The   Ordinary
Young Man is
surrounded.
Mayakovsky

If you'd lived as I've lived

You would leave off living.

You would hunger for horizons—

Crack east and crack west

Like the smoke-smeared faces

Of factories cracking

The bones of the sky.

Ordinary Young
Man

Whaddaya mean? Whaddaya mean?

Doesn't love count for something,

Doesn't—think of little Sonya,

She's my little baby **sisteR!**

On his knees

Look—let's not have any trouble.

We don't want to have a riot!

The alarm increases.
A shot rings out.
Sewer pipes slowly
begin to sing a
single note. Metal
rooftops rattle.
The man with a
long face

If you'd loved as I've loved

You would live without love.

YOU would liquidate LOVE

In the public squares

You would rape the sheepish heavens

And the milk-tooth innocent stars.

The Man with
One Ear

Your women don't know how to **love!**

They're a bunch of swollen sponges!

A thousand feet
stomp on the belly
of the public square.
The Man with the
Long Face

AND LISTEN HONEY, if you're interested—

You can cut up my soul and make a *gorgeous*
    skirt.

Boundless agitation.
Everyone crowds
around the enor-
mous woman. They
hoist her onto their
shoulders and head
for the door.
Everyone in unison.

We will go

To the place

Where they crucified our

Good old lord

We'll go crazy with the strip-tease

And we'll dance in the street

And on sin's **black** stone

We'll raise a monument to meat.

They drag the woman to the doors but the madness finally breaks all bounds. Enter The Man with One Eye and One Leg, bursting with joy. People throw with woman into a corner. The Man with One Eye and One Leg

Stop!

On the s**tree**t everybody wears a face like a burden

And the faces are all the same.

Time's an old lady, but she just had a baby,

A twisted terror. And it's starting to grow.

As the snouts of years came wriggling out

Old men went mad and **w**ould **n**ot **s**peak.

Evil thickened the c*ity*'s wrinkle S

In veins like rivers a thousand miles long.

Slowly *a horror* of rockets of hair

Were raised on the pad of time's bald head,
AND SUDDENLY

All of the things in the world went crazy.

They tore up their voices and ripped off their
    rags

As they ran, they threw away their worn-out
    names.

The windows of wine-stores splashed by
    themselves

Like Satan pawing in the bottom of a bottle.

Pants in pairs **ran away** from their tailors

Who went into shock when they saw them move

By themselves! Without butts!

Dining room **Furniture** stumbled away

Opening its twisted blackened drawers,

And underwear wept, afraid of falling

From signs that said fashion modes.

Boots looked strict and untouchable.

Stockings wiggled their holes like whores.

I *ran and ran* like a wallfull of dirty graffiti.

I lost one leg a block away—

It's still trying to catch up with me.
Why do you all of you call me a cripple?

I hate you. You're **fat-gutted**, flabby, and old.

Remember: **nowadays** nobody's left alive

Whose legs are identical.

Curtain

Act Two
Depressed
A public square in
the city of the fu-
ture. Mayakovsky,
who is now wear-
ing a toga. And a
laurel wreath. Be-
hind a door, the
sound of many feet.
The Man with One
Eye and One Leg
Ingratiatingly

Poet, poet.

They've made **you** a prince.

There's a crowd outside the door.

They're licking their fingers and asking for more.

And they're carrying containers

Of something strange.

Mayakovsky

WHAT THE HELL. Let them come in.

Enter women with
bundles, all of them
shy. Some of them
curtsey.
A Woman who
Cries Ordinary
Tears

Here.

I don't need this any more.

It's a tear.

Take it, go on.

It's absolutely *pure.*

It's absolutely *white.*

I wrapped it in silk made from the **ligh**⌐**T**

That shines from melancholy **eyes.**

Mayakovsky
He gets nervous

   I don't need it. I don't want it.

   I don't get it: what's this all about?

To the next woman

   Look at you. Your eyes are a *mess* too. Just like
      hers.

A Woman who
Cries Little Tiny
Tears

   So what? Why should I care?

   My baby boy is dying, do you think that's **fair**?

W ho's the good looking number

With the dark brown hair?

Paperboys enter in
single file, shouting

Figaro, Figaro, Figaro, Figaro, Times, Times,
Times!

A crowd gathers
begins to shout

Oh, look!

What a wild man!

Move back a bit.

Give the boy room.

Young ma N, *stop that hiccuping.*

The Man without
a Head

Eee eee eee eee!
Eh! Eh! Ehhhhhhhhhh....

e Man with Two
es

ook at the clouds, they're melting in the gold of
the sun.

're **frivolous**, they're fragile, and they're
ading fast.

But I don't care. Listen here,

Here's another little tear.

I wept it specially for you.

You *can* sew it on your shoe.

It'll be real pretty, don't you think?

Mayakovsky is
afraid
A Woman who
Cries Great Big
Tears

Don't look. I must be a mess too. A wreck.

Next time I'll be in better shape, I promise.

Anyway, **here's** a tear from m**E**.

This is not one of your everyday drops,

This is a **professional tear.** It's twice

Mayakovsky

That's enough. This is too ma

For a man to bear.

Anyway I gotta go n

But say—who's that ove.

The day is dead. All over and done.

Even the daughters of heaven are gold-diggers too.

All they want is money money money.

Mayakovsky

What? What? Who?
*The Man with
Two Kisses*

All of them do it for money money money.

*Voices from the
crowd*
Quiet! Quiet!

*The Man with
Two Kisses
He dances with a
ball full of holes*

Somebody gave two kisses to a big and greasy man.

He was all upset and he just **didn't know**

What to do with them or where to go.

It was a high old time in the CITY

Everybody singing holy *hallelujah!*

People were dressed up in beautiful clothes.

But the man *was* cold,

The **so**le**s** of his shoes had *oval holes*.

He *took* the **biggest** ki*ss*

And he *put it on*—

A kiss GALOSH.

But the cold got wise, still STUNG his toeS.

"Oh what the hell," HE said.

"I'll throw them away.

These *kisses* are good for nothing anyway!"

And t**ha**t's w**ha**t he DID.

Then all of a sudden

The little kiss **grew** ears

And started fidgeting around:

t made a teeny-weeny **sound**,

It said: "*mommy*".

The man got scared.

He wrapped the poor thing up in a piece of his
soul

And he took it home to keep it

In a sky-blue bowl.

For a long time he poked around **in dusty
trunks**

He was looking for the bowl.

Then he turned around--

The kiss was sprawled out on the couch!

It had got fat!

Fat!

It laughed a fat-mouthed laugh.

"OH GOD,"

The man cried,

"Who would have thought I'd ever get so tired!

I'll go and hang myself."

And that's what he did.

And while the poor man hung

And stunk

Women in bedrooms everywhere—

Smokestackless factories—

Kept **G**RINDING OUT millions of kisses:

Big kisses

Little kisses

All kinds of kisses

With the fat-flesh levers of their smacking lips.

*Enter a crowd of
kids dressed as
kisses; they speak.*

They sure made a lot of us kisses! Hooray!

Take me, I'm yours!

Hey! There's more of us coming, hundreds every
        day!

HEY! MY NAME IS MICKEY!

Let's make it. ok?

*They pile up a
heap of tears in
front of the poet
Mayakovsky.*

Mayakovsky

Ladies and gentlemen, I'm just about through.

This is **breaking my heart** again and again,

Taking these tears.

If you only knew.

None of this seems to bother any of you.

But what about me and my pain?

Shouts from the crowd

That's *your* problem!

You keep it up with the fancy *talk*

And you'll always wind up in hot water!

The Old Man with One Skinned Cat Left

Sonny, you're the only one left who knowS how to write a poem.

So you just take up your burden. Haul it all back to your god.

He points to the heap of tears. Mayakovsky

Just let me rest for a minute.

They don't. He awkwardly packs up the tears in his bag. He just stands there, holding the bag.

OK, I'm done.

Just let me say goodbye.

I thought I could go on having fun forever,

I had such great big beautiful EYES—

I thought that being a prince would be heaven.

But no. It's back to gray skies

And the open road. You roads, I'll remember you
        forever—

Skinny **LEGS** moving

Toward the long gray curls of that northern river.

So this is the day

Of my great GET-AWAY!

Got to get out of this cit**Y**!

I'm leaving my soul in rags and tatters

On the sharp hard edges

Of your nitty-gritty.

The moon will go with me

As far as she can; to a place

Where the arches of heaven crumble

And the sky falls flat.

She'll glide up beside me and idle for a moment

While she tries on my derby hat.

Then I'll shoulder my bundle and keep on **haulin G**

I may fumble and fall and wind up crawling

Just a stumblebum with a heavy burden

But I'll keep on moving further and further

North,

Where the world is locked in a vise of ice,

In a frozen spasm of eTeRnAl despair,

And the icy fingers of fanatical oceans

Claw for the heat of its heart. And I swear,

I swear, I'll make it there.

I may be ExHaUsTEd

But my last mad gesture

Will be for you all: I'll throw your tears

In old grim-god's face

In his primal prison,

The source

      of the sign

           of the beast.

          Curtain

Epilogue
Mayakovsky

LADIES and *gentlemen,*

I wrote all this myself.

It's about poor suckers

Like you.

Too bad I don't have tits.

I could gi**ve** you a mouth**ful**

Like your **G** ood old mama used to do.

But I'm really sucked dry.

And *now* you know why.

Anyway, I'm through.

I may seem like a simple-minded idiot to you.

But on the other hand, think of it this way:

Who else could provide

S uch a **SUPERHUMAN** avalanche of
argumentation?

What happened was, God opened his heavenly

MOUTH

And I put my foot right in it. Told him

I was his greatest creation.

There are times when I think I'd like to be a
    great artist—

You know, like Rimsky-Korsakov,

Or maybe become famous overnight, like
    Tchaikovsky.

But whenever I really think about it seriously

I like my OWN name best—

VLADIMIR MAYAKOVSKY

*

Vladimir Vladimirovich Mayakovsky was born in 1893 in the village of Bagdadi, near Kutayis (now renamed Mayakovsky) in the Republic of Georgia. At the age of twelve Mayakovsky experienced the first Russian Revolution and the death of his father. In June of 1906 his family moved to Moscow, where he entered high school and was brought into political work with the then Russian Social Democratic Workers' Party (Bolsheviks). He became a member of the party the following year.

The next years saw a great deal of political activity, as he was arrested and released several times. In 1911 he passed the entrance examination for the training college of painting and fine arts and entered a class for figure painting. Over the next few months he met David Burliuk and several poets of the Futurist Group, including Velimir Khlebnikov, Alexei Kruchonykh, and Vasily Kamensky. In 1912 he joined Burliuk, Khlebnikov, and Kruchonykh in the manifesto A Slap in the Face of Public Taste.

In November of the next year he rehearsed and presented his first play Vladimir Mayakovsky: A Tragedy *at the Luna Park theatre in St. Peters-*

burg. Over the next few years he wrote some of his major works, including "A Cloud in Trousers," "Man," and his play Mystery Bouffe *(1918)*. Most of these works were written in support of the new Soviet order, but Mayakovsky's later works, such as The Bedbug *(1928)* and The Bathhouse *(1930)* were satirical criticisms of the new order. He grew increasingly disillusioned with Soviet life and committed suicide in 1930.

CPSIA information can be obtained
at www.ICGtesting.com
Printed in the USA
BVHW062136041118
532172BV00006B/85/P